# DANCE WITH THE MOON

poems for children

*To Catrin with best wishes from Dennis Carter 7·11·07*

## by
## DENNIS CARTER

# catchfire publications

Autumn 2007

Pentre Farm, Woodhill, Oswestry,
Shropshire. SY10 9AS
phone: 01691 656320
email:
dennisbcarter@hotmail.com

ISBN 978-0-9533499-5-1

## About the author.

Dennis Carter's three previous books of poetry for children *Sleeplessness Jungle, On the Razzle Dazzle* and *Shiny Metal Words* have been big hits around the schools of England and Wales. Over 4000 have been sold so far and whenever Dennis returns to schools where he has read them out loud every child has a favourite. Dennis is very excited about his new book *Dance with the Moon* and thinks it is his very best.

Dennis started writing poems and stories for children when he was a young teacher. Even then he loved performing his work to classes and sometimes to the whole school. Now he likes reciting them and sometimes even singing them. He guarantees that you will laugh.

Dennis lives in north Shropshire with his wife and family and when he is not writing or pretending to do the garden he goes into schools to teach children how to improve their poetry-writing. He thinks all children have something important to say and can write good poems and stories.

Dennis Carter has also written two stories for children *Misspellboobiland* and *Bringing Home the Dead*, which are still available.

# ACKNOWLEDGEMENTS:

Thanks to the schools in Flintshire, Denbighshire, Wrexham, Powys, Gwynedd, Cheshire, Shropshire, Lincolnshire and Yorkshire which I have visited in recent years.

Thanks to all the children who have listened and responded to these poems. They have helped me to improve them.

Thanks to *The Guardian* newspaper for the news story 'Lovelorn Jake's 8-mile duck walk' on 25.3.05 which I used for *Jake's Journey* and for the news story 'Mystery of seal found stranded in a country lane' on 1.12.06 which I used for *Sidney the seal.*

Thanks to *The Daily Post* newspaper for the news story 'Moody monkey on run from zoo after row' on 31.5.05 which I used for *Moody Monkey.*

All poems are by Dennis Carter except *Custard Butterflies* pages 74 to 75 by Dunstan Carter.

All illustrations are by Ian Douglas except *Jake's Journey* opposite page 18 by Tom Crawford and *The Coming of the Vikings* opposite page 8 by Karmen Mitchell.

WELCOME

## WELCOME

If you're a friendly
visitor to our house

on a clear cold night
in the midwinter

wipe your feet on
the welcome mat

and come into
the draughty porch.

Pull open the old
wooden door

to our large cosy
sitting room

where you may sit
and take a drink

and hang out with
all the great stars.

# SHOPPING TRIP

Mum and Dad and
Dad and Mum
went to the shops
with Rumbling Tum.

They bought buns,
they bought cake,
they bought sweets
and made Tum ache.

They bought chocolate,
they bought coke,
they bought crisps
and made Tum choke.

They bought burgers,
they bought fries,
they stuffed Tum
up to his eyes.

They let him chew,
they let him lick
till Rumbling Tum
was very sick.

# DON'T DANCE DAD
*(for Beatrice)*

It began the night of the school disco,
the kids were feeling sweaty and frisko.
Dad came early but he should have come late-
soon he did a jive instead of a wait.
Oh no!
*Here's a jiggle- jingle, jingle.*
*There's a wiggle- time to mingle.*
*"Don't dance Dad!"*


In a fashion store she's trying on clothes,
music is playing, women push in droves.
She spots Dad tapping, a glint in his eye
so drops the jacket she wanted to buy.
Oh no!
*Here's a jiggle- jingle, jingle.*
*There's a wiggle- time to mingle.*
*"Don't dance Dad!"*


Down in the doctor's stuffy waiting room
Dad's ears are wagging to a radio tune.
Glum patients stare through their downcast eyes
as Dad hears number one and starts to rise.
Oh no!
*Here's a jiggle- jingle, jingle.*
*There's a wiggle- time to mingle.*
*"Don't dance Dad!"*

The football match is heading for a draw
but the striker strikes and the home crowd roar,
out booms "I feel good" as the whistle blows.
Too much and with a wriggle off Dad goes.
Oh no!
*Here's a jiggle- jingle, jingle.*
*There's a wiggle- time to mingle.*
*"Don't dance Dad!"*

It's holiday time and the flight was great!
Off to miles of beach, not a minute late.
But in the flash hotel collecting our keys
tinny music starts up and gets to Dad's knees.
Oh no!
*Here's a jiggle- jingle, jingle.*
*There's a wiggle- time to mingle.*
*"Don't dance Dad!"*

## SPRING 1

Whiteness
along hedgerows
makes a merry-go-round
around fields, dressing them up for
summer.

## CLOUDS

Who wipes
Sky's blue and white
to make them shine?

*Wind's puff fluffs them up.*
*Sun's gleam beams them clean.*

Who's turned
sky into sea with
frothed up waves?

*Wind's puff fluffs them up.*
*Sun's gleam beams them clean.*


## HIT AND RUN
## VICTIMS

Sad and forlorn
is the badger,
the hedgehog,
rabbit and red fox,

lying at the side
of the road,
hit and run
victims all alone.

Nobody feels
sorry for them,
nor even whispers
a quiet prayer.

Have you seen
a tear being shed
or heard a voice
say "Ah poor things"?

Shambling badger
in the twilight,
hedgehog rolling
into a ball;

rabbit frozen
in headlight's glare
or rushing fox
running headlong;

they die, never
seeing the danger,
next day lying there
dashed and damp.

Who knows how long
they took to die?
Feel and mourn for
all these creatures!

# LITTLE LIAM JONES

Little Liam Jones
forever he moans
morning and noon and night.

If it's not his nose
it'll be his toes
or an itchy insect bite.

If it's not his eye
it'll be the cry
of foxes in the wood.

It it's not a wart
it'll be the thought
of the red of his own blood.

If it's not his tongue
it'll be his lung -
he's always out of breath.

If it's not his ear
it'll be his fear
of a very painful death.

# THE COMING OF THE VIKINGS

Over-crowded on a broken
gravestone seven weapon-wielders:

the seven huge-eyed, the seven
hook-nosed in Death's long procession.

Vikings bringing the flashing
lightning, fiery dragons and famine.

Vikings breaking churches and
breaking bones in A.D. 793.

For seven years then the seven
young monks wandered Northumbria,

lambs escaping wolves the seven
chosen ones with Cuthbert's treasures:

those glittering gospels, Oswald's
head and the bones of St Aidan.

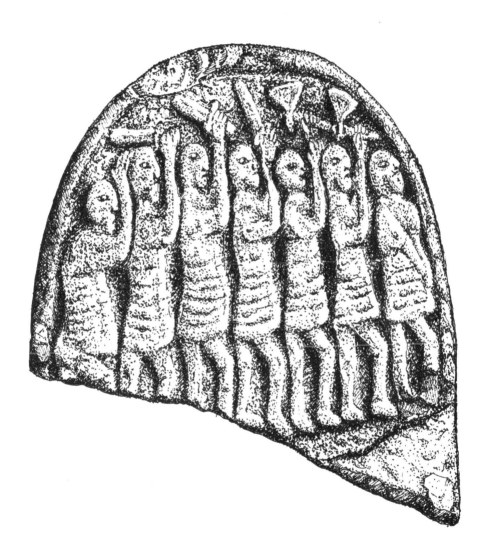

# A WINTER RIDDLE

As we walked towards
the distant hill, was
it or wasn't it snow

just before the frozen
air rubbed out the trees,
the fields and the hill?

Close by us a fir tree
was filigreed with frost
like finest lace;

under our feet the ground
was as solid as a
dinosaur's bones.

Above our heads next spring's
buds were gloved or
bonnetted with hoar frost

and thick white moss grew
fluffy over the wires,
blunting every barb.

But was it or wasn't it
snow on that far
hill getting closer?

9

When sun picked out
a row of trees, making
silver castings of them

then marked out
the boundary of one field,
turning it to wobbly tin

we knew the answer.
Was it or wasn't it snow?
No, the thickest frost

and if you scraped
some up you suddenly
held a shiny snowball!

## BIRTH OF THE MOON

Surely the moon slips now
through a slit in the sky.
Its coin will roll in the till
but what will it buy?

Or perhaps an eyelid
lifts from a silvery eye
that watches the sad world
with never a cry.

## MAGIC PRISM

*Magic prism please tell me*
*a story before I go to sleep.*

Here is a story little one,
a story to make you dream:

One night blue bubbles popped over
red balls and all was purple.

One morning yellow cymbals clashed
over blue stones and I saw green.

One evening red puffballs burst on
yellow grass and orange was born.


## WHY SAID

Why said to his brother Can
"What do we need to make a man?"
Can said to his brother Why
"Bits and pieces six feet high."

# HOT AIR BALLOONS

Hot air balloons
sail along stately:
distant dragons lifting
higher their roaring fire.

Hot air balloons'
slow exclamations
punctuate the sky with their
bright coloured lightbulbs.

Hot air balloons
carry their cargoes
over the dull land that
slides away smoothly.


# RAINY HILLS

Rain all week went
tsssst and tsssst again

until long white threads
spun down the high hills
into the weaving river

and shshsh they went
and shshsh again.

# REMAINS OF VIROCONIUM

Wandering through remains
of Viroconium imagine if.....
a computer rebuilt the walls
and tied a helmet on your head
and put a sword into your hand
and strapped a shield upon your arm.

Wandering through remains
of Viroconium imagine if.....
a computer roofed the bath-house
and poured the steam into the baths
and laid out wine and food on boards
and floated music on the air.

Wandering through remains
of Viroconium imagine if.....
a computer turned *then* to *now*,
and bathed your exhausted body,
and fed your ravenous stomach,
and delighted your giddy brain.


### Haiku 1
Footprints of a child
side by side with a seagull's -
gull flew and child cried.

## THISTLE

Prickly green candles
of the many-branched
candlestick are lit
with purple flames

and the fuzzy bumble
bee he loves them,
nuzzling down
into their warmth.

## GOING AWAY

Going away,
they are going away,
the dog and the cat
they are going away.

Look for them here
and look for them there
you will not find them
they do not care.

## ROMAN SOLDIER

Roman soldier
marching into Egypt
what have you got?
*A short, sharp sword*
*dangling from my belt.*
*Sharp sword.*

Roman soldier
marching into Spain
what have you got?
*A long, curved shield*
*fastened to my arm.*
*Sharp sword, curved shield.*

Roman soldier
marching into Germany
what have you got?
*A shiny, round helmet*
*with wings on my head.*
*Sharp sword, curved shield,*
*round helmet.*

Roman soldier
marching into Gaul
what have you got?
*Beaten metal armour*
*rattling from my shoulders.*
*Sharp sword, curved shield,*
*round helmet, metal armour.*

Roman soldier
marching into Britain
what have you got?
*Leather strapped sandals*
*bound to feet and legs.*
*Sharp sword, curved shield,*
*round helmet, metal armour,*
*leather sandals.*

## SPRING 2

Tiny
toadlet smaller
even than a penny
or tiddlywink is hopefully
hopping.

## WHERE I WENT

I went into Pudding Lane,
ate some pudding,
came out again.

I went up to Bailey Head,
felt a little dozy,
climbed into bed.

I went along Chapel Street,
found my friend
but lost my feet.

I went over Castle Green,
fell in the lake
and came out clean.

I went under Railway Bridge,
heard a weird sound,
saw an ostrich.

I went by the old church tower,
saw a young face
but it was sour.

## JAKE'S JOURNEY
*(a true story)*

Let me tell you a strange story,
the story of lovelorn Jake,
a lively duck , a friendly duck,
and, being male, a drake.

Jake was such a handsome fellow,
feathered over in white
with a red face, a black bottom,
punk hairdo. What a sight!

He loved life in the country park,
splashing in the bright lake.
But mostly he loved Jemima,
she made his young heart ache.

Jake fathered Jemima's ducklings -
twenty three little things,
but when Jake got into trouble
the warden clipped his wings.

Then Jake could only walk not fly
and still the troubles came.
They sold him so he'd never see
Jemima ever again.

There was no time for long goodbyes-
Jake was thrown in a truck.
The truck rattled and the truck rolled.
Poor Jake was out of luck.

When it stopped he was shooed into
a farmer's mucky pool,
where the other ducks ignored him.
Jake felt a proper fool.

Now drakes like Jake don't have the skill
to find their own way home.
But he wanted his Jemima
so he left the farm to roam.

He found the road, "Which way to go?"
the words went through his bill.
He didn't dip, he simply guessed,
"I'll go this way, I will."

He waddled up, he waddled down,
he waddled days and nights
with the fast cars whizzing past him
blaring and glaring lights.

His feet were not made for walking
on bumpy tarmac lanes.
They were webbed and made for swimming
and soon were full of pains.

But Jake was tough, he just kept on
and by the third day's end
he could see in the far distance
as he came round the bend

the country park, his rightful home,
the place where he was hatched,
the lake where lovely Jemima
swam here and there and watched.

There was such a mad kerfuffle
when Jake jumped by her side.
Ducks flew here and the drakes flew there,
Jemima simply cried.

If Jake had not found Jemima
he might have pined away
and when the warden saw them kiss
he said, "Jake has to stay!"

## WHAT WOULD YOU DO
## IF THE MOON?

What would you do if the moon
were a butterfly in its cocoon?
*Order the airforce to guard the cabbages.*

What would you do if the moon
grew bright leaves and petals next June?
*Pluck it and put it on the hair of the milky way.*

What would you do if the moon
let down its wheels and went off with a zoom?
*Hitch-hike a lift to the nearest galaxy.*

What would you do if the moon
were to burst in a shower with a boom?
*Make a million pieces of cheese on toast.*

What would you do if the moon
dropped down to earth like a prune?
*Buy up the complete stocks of custard powder.*

What would you do if the moon
went blue and became a balloon?
*Invite the whole world to a special party.*

What would you do if the moon
started turning and playing a tune?
*Ask all the guests to start dancing.*

What would you do if the moon
unwound its ribbon into a festoon?
*Cut it up and throw it over the dancers.*

What would you do if the moon
shouted "Save me. Please save me soon?"
*Tell the presidents to make peace at once.*

What would you do if the moon
gave up the ghost on a grey afternoon?
*I don't know. What do you suggest?*

## THE DOTTED SEA

On the blue dotted,
yellow dotted sea,
below the red dotted,
blue dotted,
yellow dotted sky,
a fleet of fishing
boats is one reflected boat
bobbing
its hundreds of dots.

# TOADSTOOLS

*Down in*
*the wet wood*
*the wet wood the wet wood*
golf balls swelling
inky caps smelling
creamy umbrellas
on treeroot cellars
*down in the old wet wood.*

*Down in*
*the wet wood*
*the wet wood the wet wood*
sticky mouths open
on branches broken
black bubbles bursting
on creepy curtains
*down in the old wet wood.*

*Down in*
*the wet wood*
*the wet wood the wet wood*
red buttons hanging
off jackets dangling
white tops on black caps
underneath pink flaps
*down in the old wet wood.*

## CANDY IN SPRING

With your stream that
gurgles, turns and twinkles
when the morning sun
lights up your wrinkles
*Candy you're fine and dandy.*

With your wooded slopes
of birdsong bubbling,
your chicks in nests
under mother's cuddling
*Candy you're fine and dandy.*

With your woodpecker rap
and peacock butterflies,
your rustling leaves and
bumble bee mutterbyes
*Candy you're fine and dandy.*

With your long hill shadows
and buzzards gliding,
your ferny lanes and
little voles hiding
*Candy you're fine and dandy.*

With your primrose
buttons on grassy coats
that hang on hedges
right up to their throats
*Candy you're fine and dandy.*

With your pussy
willows yellow fluffing,
lambs tails dying but
your green leaves puffing
*Candy you're fine and dandy.*

With your nibbly sheep
and lambs cavorting,
walking families and
young lovers courting
*Candy you're fine and dandy.*
*Oh yes! You're very dandy!*


## SUMMER 1

Lying
still on the sand
sunbathers seem to be
hot dog sausages on slices
of bread.

## HOPELESS ROAD

When I was hopping up
Hopeless Road
I met a croakless
three-legged toad.

As I was hissing down
Silly Street
I flew away with
a flock of geese.

When I was spinning up
Crazy Lane
I bumped into
myself again.

As I was creeping down
Weirdy Way
my other self said
"Go away!"

### Haiku 2
Ripples on the lake:
tiny indicator lights
on/off/on/off/on.

# CAVE PAINTING

One bison we tracked -*Oh-jay!*
over the wide plain tracked -*Oh-jay!*
With my flowing fingers I draw
his thick hide blowing
his humped neck resting
his hard hoof scratching
his shiny eyes staring
*Oh-jay! Oh-jay! Oh-jay!*

Two horses we saw -*Oh-jay!*
with our own eyes saw -*Oh-jay!*
I pick up my sharp flint and draw
their open mouths chewing
their small heads nodding
their short manes shaking
their many legs prancing
*Oh-jay! Oh-jay! Oh-jay!*

Three mammoths we hunted -*Oh-jay!*
with our pointed spears hunted -*Oh-jay!*
I pick up my burnt stick and draw
their woolly coats ruffling
their angry tusks pointing
their heavy hooves pounding
their sorrow eyes drooping
*Oh-jay! Oh-jay! Oh-jay!*

# TARMAC MAN

Tarmac man he wears
no yellow coat but
loves his gloves, his
red rubber gloves
and when you go out
in the car he always
follows you, follows
you and if you look back
to try to see Tarmac Man
you'll never find him.
He vanishes with
the petrol fume vapours
from the exhaust pipe,
then as soon as you turn
back round to your
music or your comic
he bounces back out
of the road again with
staring eyes and double
chin, with chubby body
but most of all his rubber
gloves, his red rubber
gloves drumming fingers
on the back of your car.
That's Tarmac Man.

## WHAT IS THE DIFFERENCE?

What is the difference between
a leaf and a wren as you walk
at the edge of the autumn wood?
*Leaf drops.*
*Wren sings.*

What is the difference between
an owl and a bell up in the belfry
of the old church tower?
*Owl hoots.*
*Bell dings.*

What is the difference between
a mouse and a bat, for both
are covered in finest coat of fur?
*Mouse legs.*
*Bat wings.*

What is the difference between
a worm and a snake, for each writhes
and wriggles in the earth and grass?
*Worm shines.*
*Snake stings.*

What is the difference between
November and March, for in either
the cold wind sneaks through your coat?
*November takes.*
*March brings.*

What is the difference between
a walking stick, a heron's beak,
a magic wand, a wooden spoon,
a boomerang, a cricket bat and a hammer?
*What a question!*
*Many things.*

## SPRING BANK

All winter long
that poor old bank
at the side of the lane
shivered in rags
shivered in tatters.
Now spring
has come and put
a green coat on his back
and down his arms
and buttoned it brightly
up with primroses.
In summer though
won't he be too hot?

## IN THE RAIN FOREST

Deep in the dazzling rain forest
I am lost, I am lost!
Submerged in bootlace creepers
Will I drown, will I drown?

Pelted by curly leaves, spattered
by yellow parrot droppings,
stared at by scarlet eye-flowers
I am lost! Will I drown?


## FEED THE CAT

A plaintive miaow from
a sad-looking face
that says, "Please feed me."
Grab the latest blue

supermarket tin:
'Turkey chunks in Jelly'-
reads like a special treat
at Christmastime.

She's going to love this
so pull of the lid.
It smells of muck- spreading
or something stuck

to the sole of a shoe,
the cat's dinner.
She sidles purring
past, crouches, gobbles.

How could she eat that?
But I remember
the rabbit she ate,
crunching through the skull,

snaffling every bit
but for the bob tail
and shiny bowel.
She eats it all right!


## JACKDAW TANKA

In flocks the jackdaws
across a fading sunset
make their ways darkly

with cackling conversations
finding their roosting branches.

# TUMBLING RUMMY

*Listen to your tummy.*
Here's a train screeching
through a tunnel in
the dark, without a
driver or a horn.
*Tumbling rummy, rumbling tummy.*

*Listen, listen to your tummy.*
In the deep distance
a baby's wailing.
Somebody feed it
or bring up its wind!
*Tumbling rummy, rumbling tummy.*

*Listen to your tummy.*
Have you ever heard
a sewing machine?
Here it comes again,
stitching your stomach.
*Tumbling rummy, rumbling tummy.*

*Listen, listen to your tummy.*
Was that a grey wolf
howling to the moon,
hungry and alone
down in the forest?
*Tumbling rummy, rumbling tummy.*

*Listen, listen to your tummy.*
An ambulance squeals,
making us all move,
in a wild hurry
along city streets.
*Tumbling rummy, rumbling tummy.*

*Listen to your tummy.*
Or funny little
bubbles like bats pop
and flutter into
the cave of your mouth.
*Tumbling rummy, rumbling tummy.*


## SUMMER 2

Swaying
in their dresses
warm cheeks and hands on hips
a huddle of trees in the breeze
gossips.

## TEENAGE BROTHER

In bed all day long.
Wakes up, screams a song.

His head's in a cloud.
He plays rap loud.

From his mouth loud swears
as he bangs downstairs.

Mum shouts, "You're rude!"
He replies, "Thanks dude."

His face is not clean.
To me he is mean.

Weird face, eyes twitchin',
Scares me in the kitchen.

Burnt toast in toaster.
Sexy girl on poster.

Often drinks Dad's beers.
Smiles and says, "Dad, cheers!"

Stays out very late.
Down town with his mate.

## THE POOL

*Nicholas jumps the pool.*
*Nicholas jumps the pool.*
*Emma steps in and*
*Lindsay wades in and*
*Nicholas jumps the pool.*

The pool is dark
with the rain clouds in it.

The pool is meshed
with the beech tree on it.

The pool now shines
with the car's lamp on it

*and Nicholas jumps the pool.*
*Nicholas jumps the pool.*
*Emma steps in and*
*Lindsay wades in and*
*Nicholas jumps the pool.*

The pool now frowns
with the child's shoe in it.

The pool makes rings
as the splash lands in it.

The pool now sings
as the splash jumps from it

*as Nicholas jumps the pool.*
*Nicholas jumps the pool.*
*Emma steps in and*
*Lindsay wades in and*
*Nicholas jumps the pool.*


## NIGHT

Night breaks soft waves
of cloud on the red shore

and flushes out flocks
of silver starbirds.

Night strings a single
pearl on the tree's neck

and one in the lake
that melts and wobbles.

# THE WOOD SPIRIT

Spirit of the woods,
my long hair trailing,
among the trees I float,
leaves my ceiling.

If you wish to see me
tread so quietly
on the bristly cones
and beetles shiny.

Spirit of the woods,
keen eyes staring,
I skim the ragged ferns,
shadows my flooring.

Never snap a twig
or a leaf crackle
for then I will vanish
with a quiet cackle.

## LAMB AND
## SHEEP TALK

*Beeeehr*
Where are you mummy?
I need a drink.
*Baah*
Over here as usual,
what d'you think?

*Beeeehr*
What's the grass taste
like under that tree?
*Baah*
Come chew it for
yourself - don't ask me.

*Beeeehr*
This grass is hopeless,
yellow and dry.
*Baah*
Do you expect the grass
ten feet high?

*Beeeehr*
Is that the farmer
blowing his horn?
*Baah*
Don't be silly a
cow's in the corn.

*Beeeehr*
Look at me leaping
such a great height.
*Baah*
Little lamb settle
down for the night.

## DRAGONFLY

Delicate crackle
of dragonfly's cling
film wings reveals her
as she hovers down
to the flat weeds to
dot and dab eggs from
her slim bottom as
if decorating
a child's sweet cake with
'Happy Birthday'in
dragonfly writing.

## TOUCH THE SCREEN

*Touch the screen and*
*make things happen.*
*Things disappear*
*and things come back.*

But in my dream I was
touching my face:
my nose tumbled off
and never came back;

my eye buzzed away
like a bumble bee;
my mouth it went pop
like a burst balloon;

my ear wiggle
waggled into a moth;
my hair joined the grass
blowing in the wind.

*Touch the screen and*
*make things happen.*
*Things disappear*
*and things come back.*

## WHAT DID
## THEY SEE?

Her and him
and he and she
what did they see
below the tree?

They saw a dog
bury his bone.
They saw a cat
on her mobile phone.

## MUM AND DAD

Mum, Mum
where is my ball?
Dad, Dad
where is my fiddle?
Mum, Mum
I'm going to fall!
Dad, Dad
there's a hole in
my middle!

## PASS THE REMOTE

*Pass the remote!*
Three bright red eyes
are blinking underneath
an expressionless
face, then my finger

pushes a silent
button: "Nnn-nnnnk!" says
the face and in bright
colour a man comes,

yakking about rucks
of sprawling red men
wrestling the yellows
for a large brown egg.

Soon that finger does
it again, halting
the talk in midword
and ending the fight.

The frantic talk turns
to song as the girl
in the spangles bites
a silver apple.
*Here, have the remote!*

## MY NAN

Nan, my nan, my plump
little five foot nan,
lovely and sweet
as an apple dumpling

always waiting for
me, in all weathers
watching and twitching
net curtains to see

me coming home to
her crinklecut chips
with fish fingers and
her warm rice pudding

to her comics from
the market under-
neath the cushion
below her tiny feet

but most of all to
her famous twinkle
and the heart-felt
cuddle of hot welcome.

# JOURNEYS

*Futah - futah - woa and woa*
life on a barge is so slow,
coming to a lock gate,
sit down, you'll have to wait -
life on a barge is so slow.

*Burrm - burrm - roar - roar*
travel's so fast in a car,
zoom down the motorway,
you're early night or day
travel's so fast in a car.

*Clicky - clicky - clack - clack*
on a train, on a track
the views disappear
whether far or near
on a train, on a track.

*Woosha - woosha - whirr - whirr*
on a plane through the air,
deep inside the giant bird
up above the curving world
on a plane through the air.

## MISTY DAY

"Miss Dee, oh Miss Dee
I don't understand.
That sneaky boy Mist
with his dirty hand

has started rubbing
my charcoal drawing.
It took me ages.
I called it 'Morning'.

Look at the hedges -
he's made them dull blurrs
and my lovely trees......
the picture's much worse!

Miss Dee, oh Miss Dee
That horrible lout,
that bullyboy Fog
has rubbed it all out.

With grubby hands he
made cows into smears
then messed up the woods -
and I'm now in tears."

## TEENAGE SISTER

Phone bills going through the roof
with her calls to Beth and Ruth,
Jenny, Steph and little Jo,
Rosie, Jess and jolly Mo.
*Purring, miaowing like a cat.*
*Many hours stuffed with chat.*

She drives us round the bend
shrieking with her freaky friends.
Her forefinger never rests,
tapping out her silly texts.
*Purring, miaowing like a cat.*
*Many hours stuffed with chat.*

One day fair, the next day red
the tufts of fluff upon her head.
Dad's eyes roll, Mum goes quiet
That short skirt - did she buy it?
*Purring, miaowing like a cat.*
*Many hours stuffed with chat.*

She goes clubbing to 'The Sun',
hardly any clothing on,
drawings on her eyes and face,
tattoos in a different place.
*Purring, miaowing like a cat.*
*Many hours stuffed with chat.*

## TEENAGE BROTHER'S BEDROOM

No matter how big
is brother's bedroom
it's so full of stuff
there's never much headroom.

The cardboard boxes
like tall skyscrapers.
Like seagull flocks float
his homework papers.

Underneath the bed
in the gathering dust
empty lager tins
and a pizza crust.

Pictures on his walls
of Liverpool winning,
scruffy mates gurning
and scantly clad women.

If you get caught there
without permission
brother will come on
a murder mission.

# FERAL CAT

Feral cat -
he's a bad one,
stalking round the gardens,
the other cats' gardens.
*He's coming to our house*
*paw by padded paw.*

Feral cat -
he's a wild one,
sneaking through the catflaps,
the other cats' catflaps.
*He's got inside our house*
*and skulks by the door.*

Feral cat -
he's a mean one,
looking out for trouble,
hissing, scratching trouble.
*He's prowling round our house,*
*and sharpening his claw.*

Feral cat -
he's a mad one,
bullying the pussies,
the fluffy, purring pussies.
*He's chasing in our house*
*poor Pegs across the floor.*

Feral cat -
he's a cruel one,
biting into cat skin,
gentle, harmless cat skin.
*He's got Peg like a mouse*
*and opens up his jaw.*

Feral cat -
he's a scared one,
scampering for his exit,
hissing with his fear.
*I've trapped him in our house*
*and he is bad no more.*


## SUMMER MAGPIES

Sleek magpie mum,
cocking her long tail, clicks
from the high green hedge
to her jumping chicks

who recently left
their raggedy home
to fly and to wander
and to roam alone.

## THE TROUBLE
## WITH IZZY

The trouble with Izzy
is the way she gets dizzy
in buses, trains and cars.
She shouts, 'I'm in a tizzy,
a tizzy, yes, a tizzy'
and then sees shooting stars.

The trouble with Izzy
is she's often too busy
to come outside and play.
She says, "I'm too busy!
I'm busy, busy, busy!
Come back another day.'

The trouble with Izzy
is she fights with Lizzie
morning, noon and night.
She says, 'I hate Lizzie,
Lizzie, Lizzie, Lizzie!
She makes me scratch and bite.'

# WIND AT NIGHT

You can moan outside.
I will not let you in.
You can run and hide
and rattle my bin.
Squeeze little pieces
of you around doors.
Make songs and sneezes
through gaps in the walls.
> Go 'Rat-a-tat-tat!'
> and chat 'Tittle-tat.'
> Go fat or go thin
> I will not let you in.

Thump down the chimney,
and barge windowpanes.
Creep dark and grimly
and gurgle the drains.
Curse under the door,
shout rude up the pipe.
Scream over the floor
or play a hornpipe.
> Go 'Rat-a-tat-tat!'
> and chat 'Tittle-tat.'
> Go fat or go thin
> I will not let you in.

You mad bag of stuff
get out of my yard!
You strut and you puff
and think you're so hard.
I refuse to hear
your bellowing slang.
You won't get in here
with your thud and bang.
> Go 'Rat-a-tat-tat!'
> and chat 'Tittle-tat.'
> Go fat or go thin
> I will not let you in.

But if you go silly,
soft-flopping about,
so daft and so dilly -
no longer a lout
I might change my mind
and open the door
and let your tail wind
and brush clean the floor.
> Go 'Purr and go 'Shush'
> like my little puss.
> Go thin and go fat
> like my favourite cat.

## RUINED CASTLE

Walk through any door-
way on your way to
mid air or the tops
of the high, high trees.

Without knocking go
into the king and queen's
room to find not a bed
but a feint breeze.

Look through the window
down the green valley
where cattle armies
are planning their siege.

When you see the tall
man who stands up straight
and wears posh clothes bow
down and say, "My liege."


**Haiku 3**
In sluggish bundles
fatsmells wrap up the chatter
in the cafeteria.

# NOVEMBER THE SIXTH

Charred circles in fields
are still smouldering.
Wind arriving makes
their red flowers bloom.

Cold cases lie dead in
the morning grass,
their hot genies freed
into the darkness.

Rockets like lost friends
lie in strange places:
hanging from an old
magpie's ragged nest,

nose-first in cowpats
or even jammed in
satellite dishes
to switch off the Sky.

Last night's become
a dimming memory
till at my window
red and purple burst.

## TO MIX COLOURS

Follow the dark blue path
though the bright red lawn
and find the purple lake.

Ride the yellow horse
along that dark blue path
into the green forest.

Climb down the red steps
and go through the yellow tunnel
into the orange cavern.

## MOON VOYAGES

One night one moon
turned into four,
four moons sailing
between bare trees
and past windows full
of darkness and stars.

This wonder was watched
by two children looking
along their noses.

## OLD LADY OF ABERDARON.

She ekes an existence in Aberdaron
a lovely old lady left by the world,
her cares like cuffs from uncaring winds
that rattle the rafters and reach out for her
as she shelters among quiet shadows of home,
a hermitage where herring gull preaches
and smart oyster-catcher tenderly courts her
with many a melancholy muttering of love.
Her cottage, an outcrop, collapses with age,
a wave's sigh away from the wall of the church
whose brow braves the breaking of the storms.

    Seclusion she seeks, seldom is abroad
so hermitage turns into hermit shell
enclosing her frailty, a fragile defence.
Threadbare lace curtains are lids for her eyes
blinking over windows, half-blind windows.
Foliage unfurls its fuller skirts,
billows about in the blaring wind
around the knees and the knobbly legs
of her old stone porch, pocked with lichens
like scars of the old pains, scabs of the new.

All is withering, is waning away.
Spars of an outhouse split and fallen
like fractured ribs, wrecked by storms,
cracked rock, ripped out mortar,
faltering structure, an ageing face
caving with concerns, countering strength
with a weakness almost wanton
underneath tiles that daily topple.

Yet her life's embers still embrace the fire,
burn intensely in a tiny bowl of light.
The flame of it flares with animation
in a shining symbol on her solid front door,
a brass doorhandle as bright as hope
polished to a core of caring and love,
explosion of joy among the geraniums.

## ON
## THE CLIFF

Puffins
three wearing masks
and such smart evening suits:
Coco and Pierrot and Crusty
waddling.

## SNOWDAY

Now fence posts have put on
their judge's wigs
  *Snowday, glowday,*
  *Happy, happy Snowday!*
bushes are white-haired
popstars playing gigs.
  *Snowday, glowday,*
  *Happy, happy Snowday!*


## SEAGULLS

Three seagulls paddling
on pinky flat toes.
Along comes a chilly wind
and off One goes.

Two seagulls wading
up to their breasts.
Here comes a frothy wave
and Two goes next.

One seagull waddling
quietly on his own.
A salty splash on the beak
and now One's gone.

## THE TALL SHED

In the field of eyes
and sinister shark
fins where the dark kiss
curl wriggles under
the cold curving moon
you will find my tall
shed but what might be
in there? Tell me that.

Maybe a blue swimming
pool, perhaps not,
or a rocket ship ready
for its great moment.
Is it a place for
locking up children?
No way! It's just a
scruffy storage space.

## OLD MAN'S
## MOUTH

Old man
peacefully yawns,
showing his deep mine where
splintered rocks hang and sticky streams
trickle.

60

## GOODNIGHT KISS

Dad kissed his little
daughter goodnight.
She wiped it off
as if it were a bite.

Dad looked sad but
didn't know what to say.
She said,"It's in my
head now anyway."

## THE PARTY

What do you want for your
birthday?" asked Mum.
"Snowman wrapping
paper and let's see ummm........."

answered the little
girl with the big smile.
"And what inside it?"
"My party and I'll

invite Zara, Tash
Adam and Tom
and Robyn and Ruth
and that naughty John."

## BAT ROOST

Woodpecker began it: found rot in a beech,
banged in his pickaxe well out of our reach.

He kept hollowing and opened a round
cave in the high tree well above the ground.

Woodpecker dug deep, too deep for his nest,
flew away, left it, lost all interest.

This cavern was not long empty, no way!
For ninety flying mice arrived to stay.

In the daytime they hang sweaty and hot,
packed tight together a heaving, squeaking lot.

Dusk turns them into a fluttering crowd,
a flicking, dipping spiral of dark cloud.

**Haiku 4**
Open the brown door
at the front of the onion
to many white doors.

## THE MILKSHAKE

"Please can I have
a strawberry milkshake?"
Asked the girl, "and an
ice-cream with a flake?"

"No," said Dad for the
umpteenth time that day.
"You've had some sweets -
your teeth will rot away."

"Say yes and I'll change
into stripes tonight,"
was her strange reply,
"and dance in the moonlight."

"What do you mean?"
Poor Dad was confused.
"My stripey shirt and shorts."
Could he now refuse?

### Haiku 5
Cut the cauliflower
deep into its stem to find
the ghostly white tree.

## MOODY MONKEY
*(a true story)*

*Moody Monkey*
*hit his brother*
*Moody Monkey*
*bit his mother.*

He lived in the zoo
but went on the run,
the naughtiest monkey
under the sun.

He climbed up the fence,
jumped onto the grass
and went to the city
on the underpass.

The old zoo keeper
was soon on the phone
and spoke to the police
with a mournful moan.

Off they went looking
up and down the streets
in the policemen's
most regular beats.

*Moody Monkey*
*crept into the park.*
*Moody Monkey*
*just as it went dark.*

He climbed up a tree
to the very top.
The police kept looking,
they would never stop.

The monkey rolled small
like a little bush.
The police shone torches
and one whispered, "Shush!"

They saw his long tail
like a fluffy rope.
The old zoo keeper
then started to hope.

They tempted him down
with some juicy fruit.
Monkey was tired and
no longer a brute.

*Moody Monkey*
*made friends with his brother.*
*Moody Monkey*
*said sorry to his mother.*

## SOME
## BODIES

Somebody
happy is laughing
outside New Look and
Going Places in Pride Hill.
The red ring of
her mouth encircles
her listening friends
in one brief,
eternal pause.

Little child
chasing out from
the shadows falls to
the cobbles, rattles her elbow
and breaks into tears.
The world cries too,
until a strolling
somebody comes
with a comfort.


**Haiku 6**
In the cabbage leaf
you will find the wrinkled old
face of the green man.

## STRIMMER WOMAN

Saw her buzz round
without a fear swooping,
short shorts, bright shirt,
floppy hat drooping.
*Strimmer Woman!*

She made the pure air
smokier and smokier.
She made the night
worker want to choke her.
*Strimmer Woman!*

Saw her whizz round
like a frantic robot
turning a thistle
into a do-nut.
*Strimmer Woman!*

She made the tall weeds
look so very nice.
She made mincemeat
out of the little mice.
*Strimmer Woman!*

Saw her fuzz round
in big shiny goggles,
looking like a frog
without her froggles.
*Strimmer Woman!*

She made the songs
in the beaks of birds die.
She made me think
of repeated gunfire.
*Strimmer Woman!*

## SEA WIND

Sea wind blows
the grass blue.
Sea wind blows
the trees green.
Sea wind chops
the sea into blue chips.

Sea wind froths
the pink foam.
Sea wind froths
the grey sand.
Sea wind smacks
the sea to scars of black.

## WHAT SHALL WE DO?

One, two
what shall we do?
Three, four
roll on the floor.
Five, six
play silly tricks.
Seven, eight
go to school late.
Nine, ten
whistle and then
Eleven, twelve
tickle ourselves.

## FUNNY FEET

There is a man
lives down our street

who has the very
strangest feet.

One points forwards,
the other points back.

and we all call him
Back-to-Front Jack.

## THE ARTIST
*(for Ian Douglas)*

He needs his rug
and his Toby Jug
and his coloured
patterns dangling.

He needs his tunes
to fill his rooms
with heavy rock
drummers banging.

He needs his brush
to make that gush
of green hills
below cloudy skies.

To make his art
he needs his heart,
fine feelings and
wide open eyes.

## THE GOBLIN

In the green corner
of our bright classroom
where Miss puts special
things for us to see,
to touch and to smell,
in the shiny box
with words all round it
what is that weird sound?

> *It chuns and chunners*
> *chun-chunna-chunna.*
> *It jibs and jabbers*
> *jib-jabba-jabba.*

A goblin must have
hopped from a story
on the yellow shelf ,
jumped into the box
and pulled down the lid.
The goblin is trapped,
the story's empty,
no one can read it.

> *He chuns and chunners*
> *chun-chunna-chunna.*
> *He jibs and jabbers*
> *jib-jabba-jabba.*

Should I open
that shiny box? No!
I'm much too afraid.
I'll go and tell Miss,
she will free Goblin
from his little jail.
We'll hear the story
and never more hear
>  *That chun and chunner*
>  *chun-chunna-chunna.*
>  *That jib and jabber*
>  *jib-jabba-jabba.*

## DREAM

In my dream, a beach
just out of my reach,
glowing with sunset,
night near, but not yet.
A feast on the shore
of goodies I saw:
>  lovely peach juice pools
>  and strawberry fools
>  and in blueberry shade
>  the cookies home made
>  with chocolate chips
>  and warm honey dips.

## PHEASANT

a strutting
scarlet-jowelled
imbecile

rips and shreds
quietness with his
double-shriek

strikes and shocks
calmness with his
squozen squeals

then on tip-toes
flaps and batters
thin air

mad alarm system
of sudden
ravings

he is set and
primed to go
off like this

at any time
for no obvious
reason

## CUSTARD BUTTERFLIES
*(by Dunstan Carter)*

I haven't got a net
a box or a jar
but into the dining room
I roam
hunting for custard butterflies
to call my own.
Very rarely they flap
unless blown on a spoon
and very rarely they flutter
unless captured too soon.

But the expedition my friends,
the expedition is on
and when I find the custard buterflies
they soon will be gone.
For the hunt,
yes the hunt,
oh the hunt
is never a chore.
The only downside
is that I'm left wanting more,
more of the butterflies,
the sweet, creamy butterflies,
the yummy on flutter pies,
the scrummy on mutter sighs.

Bring me a farm,
a plantation,
a zoo
of custard butterflies
until my utter size
becomes a gut
of splutter cries.

## SEA VIEWS

Out of the sea
the mountains
rise: wet feet
and cold noses.

Deep in the sea
the seaweed
lies: green arms
and brown toeses.

**Haiku 7**
Across the grey wall
sun turns green bush to black net -
afternoon magic.

## SIDNEY THE SEAL
*(a true story)*

Playing happily in the sea
was Sidney the grey seal,
wetness on his twinkling whiskers
and his smile the real deal.

But Sidney's Mummy and Daddy
then left him on his own,
so Sid got very grumpy and
let out his loudest groan.

From the cool sea to the shingle
Sidney wriggled and jumped.
Away our lumpy seal lolloped,
away he gallumped.

It was such jolly fun at first
slip-slap-slopping along
over sand and over the fields
barking his happy song.

And as he bellied down a lane,
he thought, 'Hey what a lark!'
until he felt so dry and sore
down in his underparts.

Sidney slowed down and Sidney stopped,
the lollops were hurting now.
Slip-slopping was no fun at all,
all was burning down below.

The poor seal sat, the poor seal sighed
on a quiet, grassy bank
until a noisy car came by
and then poor Sidney shrank.

He shook with fear as the people
lifted him in their arms
and put him safely in the boot
despite his worried squirms.

They whispered and they stroked him
to calm away his wriggles.
Then the R.S.P.C.A. man
had a fit of giggles.

"This has to be a joke," he said,
"a grey seal on a hike!"
"Perhaps his other tricks include
riding a motorbike!"

All of them laughed but not Sidney
until he reached the waves.
Then he laughed as loud as breakers
and swam down to his caves.

Oh he bubbled and he bellowed
from this sweet paradise,
chasing dazzling shoals of herring
in deeps as cold as ice.

When Sidney popped to the surface
just like a bobbing ball
he had a twitching, silvery fish
hanging from his jaw.

And lazily sleeping on the rocks
while Sidney had such fun
were chubby Mum and blubbery Dad
under the brightest sun.

## AUTUMN 1

A flock
of long tailed tits
like fluffy lollipops
coldly flies away rattling bags
of stones.

## STORM 1

Wild winds
call, call.

Rain, hail
fall, fall.

Fresh gales
squall, squall.

Tossed trees
tall, tall,

crash down
all, all.

## STORM 2

Hold onto the lamp post
hold onto your hat
poor puss and dinner
don't worry about that.

Watch out for the chair
watch out for the phone
look after yourself or
you'll never get home.

## PAIN KILLER

A paracetomol
pinged from its tinfoil

like an asteroid
across the kitchen

to crash down in
the fluff behind the fridge.

A mouse with a headache,
nibbling stale cheese,

also lodged behind
the fridge, licked and liked

the sweet paracetomol
then dropped dead.

### Haiku 8
As from a bonfire
above the red autumn wood-
charred jackdaws swirling.

## TEENAGE BROTHER
## TAKES HIS BREAKFAST

At two o'clock on
a bright afternoon
he zombiewalks down
to the sitting room,

sticky up hair and
tangled pyjamas,
bony thin arms as if
stripped by piranhas,

dragging a duvet
across his shoulders,
banging the doors much
louder than boulders.

Somehow he finds his
way to the kitchen,
scratching and yawning,
burping and stretching,

then fills a great bowl
to the brim with flakes,
pours the cool milk and
the sugar shake-shakes.

Out of the kitchen
the scraggy boy sails
making his flakes into
long vapour trails.

He grabs the remote,
clicks onto the Sky
and finds MTV with
the blink of an eye,

then gobbles breakfast,
surrounded by mess
like a young vulture
in his scruffy nest.


## AUTUMN 2

Conker
falls from his case -
shiny his brown eye stares
as the world goes past in a blurr -
then thud!

## SEAWEEDS

Castaway puffs of
her fluffy green hair
lead us right up to
the mermaid's dark lair.

Broken strings floating
off her watery lyre
hang where she played to
her own heart's desire.

Fabrics like jade fans
drape over her door.
Inside, the brown
carpets soften her floor.

Mermaid's been busy
for over the sands
are papery skins, straps
and pretty garlands.

What is she making
and who is it for?
There's even some bubble
wrap on the sea shore.

## SLEEPY
## MORNING

In this early
morning my eyes
are bleared.

Across the wall
the window
has been smeared.

Did someone
try to rub
away it's white

as if to bring
the return of
dark night,

and mix the
hours, turning
shallow to deep

then close his
heavy eyes and
go to sleep?

# WITH THOSE HANDS

There is a man,
his name is Dave,
with hands so large
they look like spades.

And with those hands
he digs deep holes
and puts up hills
of earth like moles.

And with those hands
he builds high walls
then cups them round
his mouth and calls.

And with those hands
pulls out big trees
and eats his sand-
wiches in threes.

**Haiku 9**
In the willow tree
sits a shiny giant crow -
blown away binbag.

# KING OFFA

*Offa was a tough man,*
*a rough man, a bluff man.*
*Offa was a gruff man*
*in seven sixty one.*

Offa made the midlands into Mercia
and grew them to greatness over the years
from Tamworth in his tall wooden tower,
his capital where his gold coins were struck.
But in the west the Welshmen worried him,
invading villages and vanishing
to the hills, the heather and the high woods,
bold with their booty and brimfull with pride.

*Offa was a tough man,*
*a rough man, a bluff man.*
*Offa was a gruff man*
*in seven ninety one.*

Offa made a truce, signed a treaty
with their princes, peace with the hillmen
and built a bank so big to keep them out.
From sea to sea he stretched this wall of earth,
this fine frontier that flowed over the hills.
You may walk your way now along its route
wending into Wales, wandering England
and meeting Offa maybe in those hills.

## OI YOU!
## *WHO ME?*

Oi you!
What do you think
you're looking at?

*Who me?*
*I'm looking at*
*your funny hat.*

*Any way,*
*what on earth do*
*you have in there?*

In here?
I have three rabbits
and a hare.

## WINTER1

Under
the old oak door
the dying beech leaf sneaked
chattering in beech leaf language
"I'm cold!"

# IN OUR HOUSE

We've got too much dangle
and not enough dingle
*in our house,*
*in our house.*

We've got too much tangle
and not enough tingle
*in our house,*
*in our house.*

We've got too much jangle
and not enough jingle
*in our house,*
*in our house.*

We've got too much mangle
and not enough mingle
*in our house,*
*in our house.*


**Haiku 10**
Early summer days -
despairing father's not yet
mastered fly-swatting.

## A MESSAGE FROM
## THE TREES

Can you hear the murmur
in the dusky hazel tree?

Can you read the runes
woven with mystery?

The tree gods have a message
for you and for me.

It's something to do
with the world's destiny.

With their friends the river gods
and the gods of the sea

surely they are telling us
what we cannot see.

"You're burning the earth,"
they say, "and boiling the sea.

"You kill part of you in
killing bird, beast and tree."

# MOTORBIKE BOYS

Motorbike Boys are
wild and noisy,
razzing round the town
so very naughty!
Where do they get
the money I wonder
to buy the fuel that
makes the thunder?

Motorbike Boys are
fourteen and fifteen.
Straight after school they
get their gears shifting,
revving their engines
and blowing blue clouds,
roaring, speeding, showing
off to girl crowds.

Motorbike Boys are
cool and hardfaced,
scaring little kids
they're such a disgrace,
weaving in and out and
doing their wheelies,
never coming home
on time for mealies.

Motorbike Boys haven't
heard the word fear
and don't even wear
protective headgear.
They like to feel wind
blowing through their hair.
They love to give mums
a nasty nightmare.

Motorbike Boys woke
me up this morning
and when I ran outside
to shout my warning,
howling in the wind
"Oi you pests yer"
one of them flagged
a very rude gesture.

## COCKS AND HENS

*What am I to do?*
Chuck-chuck-chuck-chuck-
chuck-chuck-WHO?
Chick-chick-chick-chick-
chick-chick-YOU?

*Chickens you must shoo!*
Whaaaaaaaaaaai-cock-cock?
Whoaàaaaaaaaaa-hop-hop!

# THE RED GIRL

Saturated in red
the hair, face, hands,

legs of the girl
at the top of her hill,

in reverie as
the winter sunset

makes mountains black
and the day forgotten.

Indelible, she is
paused at the edge,

the road behind blurs,
ahead is unknown.

Perfectly still she
is fixed in the sun

and never looks back
at her dumb track.

## ASTRONAUT

After you've flown
beyond the skies
do you lose your
sense of surprise?

After you've stepped
onto the moon
have you discovered
heaven too soon?

After you've raced
up to the stars
do you feel bored
when riding in cars?

## WINTER 2

Bare trees
on the cold road
cast their forlorn shadows
like withered men who lost their
money.

## DANCE WITH
## THE MOON

Lean the ladder
on the heavens and climb

beyond your dreams
to the tune of a rhyme.

Cuddle the world
for she's not very well.

Kiss the dark sky
and cast a happy spell.

Dance with the moon,
feel moondust on your feet.

Juggle the stars
over the moonwashed street.

# NOTES

1. *The Coming of the Vikings* page 8.
In 793 a.d. Vikings invaded the holy island of
Lindisfarne - north of Newcastle - and destroyed the
church. Seven monks escaped, taking with them St.
Cuthbert's holy things: the Lindisfarne gospels, the
head of St. Oswald and the bones of St. Aidan, who
founded the monastery.
2. *Remains of Viroconium* page 13.
Viroconium was a Roman town now called Wroxeter
near Shrewsbury.
3. *Candy in Spring* page 24-25.
Candy is a valley in North Shropshire.
4. *Feral Cat* page 49.
Feral cats are ones that have gone wild.
5. *Old Lady of Aberdaron* page 57-58.
Aberdaron is a village on the coast of North West
Wales.
6. *King Offa* page 86.
King Offa was king of the ancient Saxon kingdom of
Mercia, which bordered Wales. He built a wall of
earth from north to south, known today as Offa's
Dyke.

# INDEX